Love Lines

Poetry to celebrate Love

By
James Brinkley

jamesbrinkley01@gmail.com

Cover Design, Artwork, Interior Graphics and Formatting by True Beginnings Publishing. To contact the publisher, please write to the address:

true_beginnings_publishing@yahoo.com

Vector Illustration Flourish courtesy of freevectors.net.
All Illustrations, Cover Art, and Text are Copyright Protected by My Original Works Reference #69474.

Ordering Information:
To order additional copies of this book, please visit Amazon, or:
https://www.createspace.com/4717887

ISBN-13: 978-0615990798
ISBN-10: 0615990797

PRINTED IN THE UNITED STATES OF AMERICA
First Printing 2014

Table of Contents

Dedication

I'd like to dedicate this book to Kiah. She has been an inspiration to me throughout the course of writing this book. When things have been at its worst for me, she has stood by my side. To say she has been my rock would be an understatement; she has been an absolute blessing.

The Faith Walk

Faith don't wait for the nonbeliever,
Faith motivates the underachiever.
God turns the meek to the eager,
Let his will be done.
Hard times fall upon all;
You're not the only one.

Life can be a rat race,
And he will give you the pace to continue the run.
As long as there's breath in your lungs
And the belief in your heart,
Then, his kingdom will come.
When things seem too bleak and out of your reach,
Here comes the sun.

Brightness is in the hands of the righteous.
Glory be held in those who are strong enough
To bask in his likeness.
Though your burdens feel the heaviest,
If you put your faith in him,
Your struggle will be the lightest.

The Blame Dance

I take the blame for her being
The influence in my poetical frames.
She can stake claim without her name being mentioned
In not one sentence.

Invisible to you and yours,
But in my heart always present,
Absent but forever a presence.
Subject of the whole paragraph,
Before the first words indent,
Now, that's relevance.

When I speak of loving her,
that's present tense.
I just compose it with such eloquence.
I make my sentences dance
A poetical two step to a beat of romance.

My Blue Print

My creative talent is highly anticipated by the masses,
No poet but I can ace poetry classes.
My blueprint is print scripted into classics,
I have got the art of pretty paragraphs mastered.

I define rhyme line design
With the knowledge of a mastermind,
And does it in no time.

Equipped with the penmanship of a literary scholar,
Words unheard of but worth more than your top dollar.
Enough to make her mate hate my half a page equals a full holla.

Not a leader of the pack, at all,
But if they're smart, they would lace up tight
And take this blueprint and follow.

A Queen

She's a love song in physical form,

The main ingredient of a poem since the day she was born.

She took my world by storm,

And for the loving she gives my heart so longs.

A Queen in reality,

With the beauty of greatly imagined fantasy,

Sex appeals unreal so knowledgeable of her classy.

Worthy of her infinite worth;

You can't devise a way to multiply her worth,

You can't add enough numbers to math to equal her.

Unbelievable,

She makes achievable,

Because that's what she be absolutely undeniable;

A true Queen.

The Eyes Of An Angel

In the eyes of an angel I have seen heaven
And all the glory that it consists of.

I've found a focal point for all this love that I possess.
My search for that diamond in the rough has come to an end;
I have started a new beginning.

You can't get tired of winning with love like this.
You look forward to giving, because it's never too much.

For I have been touched by an angel.
There's affection from every angle, and it's so amazing.

In the eyes of an angel
I'm focused on love,
And I can't help gazing upon this beautiful angel.

My Heart Pumps Tears

Who says a heart ain't suppose to cry?

Not I.

Not when the love of your life tells you goodbye.

Not a tear comes to my eyes, but my heart pumps tears.

There's an emotional breakdown happening in there,

And I can't control the flow.

When you beg her to stay, and yet, she still says no

And now you must let go of what you once held so very tight.

Love is to be cherished, not thrown away.

So, love is worth fighting for,

But yet, my heart pumps tears.

My heart doesn't want to cry, anymore,

But how can you stop it when it's missing what it actually beats for.

The one I adore my Queen mi amore

My love runs deep; my love comes from the core,

But now, my heart only pumps tears.

She Knows Who She Is

Boy to man by your hand he has been molded,
You're a hell of a mom and you continue to show it.

You don't need my words you already know this,
A role model for a boy in his father absence.

Being a parent is a challenge but being both can be stress,
So, it's a sign of your greatness that you've passed every test.

As a mom you're the best in the position of dad you are nothing less,
And your son has been blessed to be born of you.

Not a man in this world can dismiss what you do
And all that you've done.

And if there's a woman in this world
That can make a great man of her son.

With God as my witness he made you that woman in you.

You Are Simply The Best

You've never been called daddy,

Yet you've had to play his role.

You didn't make the boy by yourself,

Yet you had a man to mold and a daughter to raise.

You bust your ass so you deserve the praise

On what is suppose to be his day.

You showed me the way;

What to do and what to say,

And how my actions were a reflection of home put on display.

I thank God for you and all that you do and all that you did,

The comfort you provided for me and my sister to live.

All the love that you gave and continue to give.

I'm so appreciative and absolutely blessed,

So, I write this to say on what is suppose to be his day

That mom you are simply the best.

She Is

My pen pulls the strings of the heart.

If paper was an instrument I guess would I play the harp;

Or maybe the guitar.

On a quest for my piece of heaven,

So, I'm shooting for my stars,

And by far it's obvious she plays a major part.

Every word combined to create these poetic lines

Are within her in mind, she is my whim, everyday sunshine.

Molded by the divine himself,

No amount of dividends nor diamonds can equal her wealth.

Worth more to me than the most precious things that this earth can offer,

Yet, no line I'll ever design will do true justice to her,

For she is far above the rest untouchable,

Yes she is simply the best.

Do I

How do I know I love her?

Well my mind tends to wander, and she's the focus like no other.

I want to cover her life with an abundance

Of happiness and emotional bliss.

Her kiss is the first, second and third wish on my list,

I crave the taste of her presence.

In her absence,

It's become evident that in this life of mine,

She's become most relevant.

Oh, believe she's been heaven sent,

In my chapter by Gods own hand,

her name's been written with pen.

How do I know I love her?

She's not quite out of my sight,

And I can't wait to see her again…

I know I love her....

Does She See

I wonder if she ever reads my sentimental sentences,
Does my preparation of words ever get seen by those beautiful eyes?
I create my inventions with the intentions of her viewing pleasure.
Each treasure uncovered for the love of her,
Emotionally painted pictures through the art of word.
Written in the penmanship and knowledge of a scholar,
As sweet as a whisper but with the impact of a holla.
Does she see my songs poetically scripted, or did she miss it,
I'm in love more than that I'm gifted,
And I write the words, so she can see and read
The words from my heart for her.
God gifted me with an angel in my life,
That's my inspiration to write, so I thank her,
But does she see my ode to a Queen,
Or does my dreams make for a reality that goes unseen.

I Apologize

Baby, I'm sorry for not being all that I can be
And what you deserve.
I promise you progression besides my affection,
And that's my word.
They say actions speak louder than words,
So, I'm going to put my action into motion.
That's the loudest talk that you've ever heard.
A Queen should be served in a manner that doubles her worth.
I want to give you the world even if it means me walking this earth.
Part of my career as your King is to subtract from your work
And dismiss, all your hurt,
Making love is a main focus, so you no longer have to search.
So with true love in my eyes, I sincerely do apologize,
And I will better, myself, to be your hell of a guy.

In The Name Of Beauty

Beauty isn't her name,

But she sure as hell can stake claim to it.

If perfection is unreachable,

She has to be as close as you can get.

Naturally, she has captured me;

Beautiful is the only way to describe her kind of pretty.

Hypnotized by feline eyes;

The things I say about her should come as no surprise.

Poems, alone, would never set the tone,

For she is the lyrics to love songs.

Born to this world in angelic form,

Add her to this life of mines, and I can't go wrong.

Powerful Beauty

Black face so beautiful,

With different shades under one beautiful race.

Designed to eat sunshine,

For you are the cream of planet earth.

Stripped of your true worth,

But you've never become worthless.

Fear gets struck within your mere presence,

But you're the absolute essence of love and affection;

Not to mention a planet built from your invention.

Someone else's name signed to your intentions,

But you were made for this.

The strength to handle the weight of the world

And not even slip is a gift.

Black face, you are powerful,

And you don't even know your strength,

And that's what's makes you so powerful.

Thank You

Wow, I get thanked for being what I'm supposed to be;

A gentleman.

Ladies no need to thank me for being what I'm supposed to be;

A gentleman.

Ladies, no need to thank me,

For I was groomed by a woman on how to love a woman completely...

I say what you all love to hear,

Because it needs to be told.

It doesn't take any intellect to call a women a bitch,

But it's the smart man who's willing to ignore the perception

That has been placed before him,

And still with a soft gentle voice express his love for his woman.

So, look her in her eyes and tell her how you truly feel,

Because there are other JPB's out here

That will tell her what her ears want to hear,

And what her heart craves to be said,

And what her body wants to feel.

Perfection

I flirt with my fantasy
On king size sheets,
I cure my cravings for sweets
With a Queen as my treat.
Beauty in abundance
From hair well done to pedicured feet.
The most beautiful thing in this world
Stands right in front of me,
Oh, only if my eyes could speak.
They would tell a tale of perfection in the form of a female,
Physically fine
By The Almighty's design.
Picture pure beauty poetically penned
In script written literature,
And that's just the outline.
Painted in the colors of a botanical garden,
A masterpiece displayed body,
Mind and soul a one of kind made just for me.

I'm Ready

If perfection is within reaching,

She's the one who should be teaching.

She's my voice of reason,

So, I pay full attention when she's speaking.

I've found love in this woman I've got,

So, I'm no longer seeking.

Affection overflows, and words show,

Emotions stay leaking into sentences turned to poetry.

I rhyme with reason; her love gives me reasons to be here.

These feelings we share are clear

And can't be compared to anything average.

We're together like marriage.

The only thing missing is my mission

To weigh her hand down with white gold and carats,

That is if she will have me.

Mold Me

Lord, mold me into the man that my lady deserves.

Make me the everything that equals her worth,

Let me be the end of the search.

I don't want to be a band-aid; I want to be the end of the hurt.

A career that consist of overtime love,

Not just a part time job to make things work.

Give me the strength to be able to hold her down

When she requires me to lift her up.

Fill my heart with sensitivity and emotional stability,

So, she knows any request is never too much.

Render my touch as soft as a kiss with GPS guidance,

So there does not exist a spot I can't miss.

I pray for the compassion to fashion

Myself the man that she has only imagined.

A dream made real not just by vision

But by something she can actually feel.

New Beginnings

I wrote a whisper for her ear,
And its destination was her heart.
My intentions are always pure and affectionate;
As her man, I play my part.
I've been about good loving right from the start,
And believe me, there's no ending in sight.
I've made love to this woman, constantly,
And that's my one and only plight.
I'm so in love with her and her life,
And that's not just because she
Added me into her beautiful space,
She's given her tender heart to me,
And I was more than willing to win it.
I've been living for more than a minute,
But she has made every minute new;
Every breath I take feels like my life's just beginning.
My God has placed an angel in my life,
And now, heaven is my ceiling.

My Fate

She's oh so much more than the allure of what you see,

But she's all that I adore; you can see that by looking at me.

I've got this glow in my eyes when she's by my side;

Her natural beauty makes my nature rise.

She be the seed that makes my love tree grow,

Every leaf is a sign that lets me know.

God don't make mistakes, and he took his time

To create a woman who's great

With the strength of an ocean

Deep as the sea, the flow of a river

But as steady as a lake.

I'll give all that she can take,

She holds me down,

So I can carry our weight without stress,

But wait with this kind of message,

Then, happiness is my fate.

Love Lessons

The love of a woman
Isn't always the whispers of sweet nothings in your ear.
It isn't always those caring words
That you want to hear and what needs to be heard.
Her arms are not always going to have comforting hands
That hug you as her man.
Sometimes, those hands will be that slap in the head
That's conformation of the things that she's constantly said.
You can't read into what was written
If it's never been read.
If she loves you things won't always be perfect
Because love consist of imperfections.
Love's not only the feel of those tender connections
Sometimes it's a push of motivation and much needed redirection.
Love and affection is worth the attention that needs to be paid
To every word that she mentions.
If she loves you, you will get all of her attention,
Whether you wanted it
If she gives it appreciate her love lessons.

Show Her Love

If you love her, be a man and say it.

If you truly love her, do the grown man thing and display it.

Your delay of it may open the door for him and them.

She must have love for you to give up on the courting of many men.

Make her your homie, your lover and friend.

Erase all of the possibilities for anyone to contend.

A heart that's not broken doesn't need to be mended.

True love's not oil and water; it's meant to be blended.

It's meant to be shared by two people who care

And part of you showing that is having your ass there.

Quality time is valuable time.

Keep on forgetting that;

Trust your replacements in line.

Always

I'll always love you, forever and a day.

For you are so amazing that I love you in so many ways.

I've got so much to say when it comes to you.

There's nothing in my world with more worth or value to me.

It's so very clear to see, that baby,

You've become my everything,

My everywhere and anything.

To make you my life,

I'll put a star on a ring.

This is my heart that you hear;

Sing this ballad to my Queen.

My love and affection sent in your direction,

Baby, by any means.

Anyway and anywhere I've produced this love,

And with you I share.

Tender love and care will always be there.

Forever and a day this I dare say:

I'll always love you.

New Management

How can a man manage to mismanage
Love management?
I was made by the man above
To handle life's challenges.
This love I've got is full of love advantages.
If love is a house; I've signed my last mortgage.
No holding back an abundance of affection;
No love shortage.
She's my moment in time,
And I'll spend each one telling her how much I adore it,
No for sale signs will be going up, here.

Your Blessing

Hold her like she means the world to you,
Cherish the moments like you want her
To be by your side for each one that you go through.
Make her an intricate part of what you do,
And that beautiful woman will become an extension of you.
Love her with actions that follow the words,
Make the term 'I love you'
The most important thing she's ever heard.
Treat her as a Queen as you know she deserves,
For she will be all that you need;
That's the purpose she serves.
If she is what you perceive a blessing,
Don't just show her and tell her she is;
Make her believe.

I'm Me, You Wanna Be Me

I'll be her full meal,

When you're just feeding her snacks.

I am the full body message,

While you're reluctantly rubbing her back.

I'm the right next to her,

When you're the where the f**k she at.

I'm love making on all four corners of the bed,

And you're just a roll in the sack.

I'm poetical on my own,

While your quotes are on loan from the Mack.

I'm a tender kiss to her lips,

And you're a back handed slap.

I'm the whisper that tells her I miss her;

You're profanity lace words that continue to diss her.

I will be what she needs,

And you be what she's got,

You gets the cold shoulder,

I gets called when she's hot.

You keep being who you are,

And I'll strive to be what you're not.

She's Going My Way

I've been loving this woman since I started liking her.
I remember the moment it took for those feelings to occur,
And where we were and the time of day.
Now, I seem poetical, but then didn't have shit to say.
I just placed myself in the way she walked every day,
And one day got the heart to talk.
Game wasn't tight,
But approached polite with the time it took
To get up the nerve had to get this right.
So, I said good afternoon at 8 in the morn.
Had an instant sense of failure coming on,
But with a smile that could light up a room,
She said, "Good morning, love; you said good afternoon."
"Oh, my bad," convo started with a laugh,
She was headed to the train station, and she's walking my path.
Man, she's going my way every day on Utica Ave.
The Manhattan Bound.

A Gift From God

No Christmas tree.

No, there was no birthday card,

Yet a value can't be placed on your worth in my life,

For you are a gift from God.

Your presence has been a present to my present,

And the future looks bright.

The clouds have been removed, and I've unwrapped my sunlight.

When there seemed to be no hope, nor a wish,

God answered my prayers with the most beautiful gift.

When things fell down, I got my uplift, and I cherish it.

So thankful am I for this gift you can't buy,

How amazing is a gift from God that can stand by your side.

I Can Be All That I Am

You are the stars on the clearest night.

You are the moon lit up so bright.

You are my sunshine.

You bring light to my days.

You are so amazing in so many ways.

You make it so easy to give you the praise.

Although I don't always show it,

I believe you are a blessing to me.

There was a space in my circle of life,

And you made it complete.

How I love you is easy to see, for you are a Queen

In the form of an angel, oh so heavenly.

God doesn't make mistakes, so how can I not believe

That you have been sent for me.

For self, I'm but a soldier, but as we, I am an army,

And with you by my side,

I will have no choice but to be all I can be.

My Perfect Picture

I use words to cover my canvas.

The picture is of a Queen born into the life of a princess.

A poetical painting of God's gift,

Just being in her presence gives my heart a lift.

So influential in my penmanship;

As beautiful as a rainbow's glow when it's sunshine lit.

My color of her lovely is not overdoing it.

It's absolutely legit.

I use the abuse of words to cosign it,

Line after line just happens to define a picture of perfection,

Painted in a paragraphs design.

W.O.W

My lady is a W.O.W.

A Woman Of Worth!

She's been that since birth.

She's grown into her greatness.

Her substance equals high maintenance.

She's most valuable to me.

Beauty in abundance as far as the eyes can see.

The shine she displays clears up my rainy days,

And she never fails to amaze.

To say she's hot isn't a lot she's Jane Blaze,

On top of her game, always and never fades.

As bright as sunlight during days,

And as beautiful as a full moon on the clearest night.

Yes my lady is W.O.W.

She's Bad shit.

She's out of sight.

Our Bond

I'll cherish each moment, so that we can build a lifetime.

This I promise with my heart, soul and mind:

To love you have I more than willingly cosign.

Line by line I design a picture of love and happiness,

And too, that I confess I'll serve you my best.

From the birth of us until I'm laid to my rest,

I'll improve on this good love and make it the greatest.

God made this for us to build upon.

This glue that is me and you has become the ultimate bond.

We are in tune with our two steps,

We are the words to our own love song.

You're the rhyme in my poems and the thoughts in my head

When I'm all alone.

Check Mate

She's my reality check,
Just because I put things in my perspective
Doesn't mean that she doesn't put my ass in check.
Recently, my life has consist of X's, negative marks,
And though she loves me,
She's not gonna cover them up with undeserved checks.
Respect begins with self,
And the cards that I've been playing aren't the cards that I've been dealt.
She's exposed my hand and has reminded me of my wealth.
Simply put, I've lost my self.
My lady saved me by putting a mirror in front of me,
So that I can see not what I was but who I've become.
Greatness is what I've sought out to be,
But in the process found the life of a bum, but she's willing to build.
A woman of substance,
A foundation but unwilling to stand still.
Elevation is consistent
Which makes me believe that she's been heaven sent.
The things that I deemed most relevant have become irrelevant,
For she's shined a light in my life of her relevance.
Who I've become, to him, I say his existence is now past tense.
The new chapter or my life begins
With an indent of a brand new paragraph and a positive sentence.

My Sunshine

If you've never seen happiness,

Look at my face when I'm talking to my lady.

Maybe, I'm a little crazy,

But she brightens my life like sunshine,

That's my baby.

No matter how my day be,

It gets much better when we share a laugh, together.

A smile from her face is an embrace,

Like the hug of a warm sweater in cold weather,

She's a love getter.

And I lets my love get her

Through my actions and these love letters.

To get her to show that smile, it's worth my while,

For her happiness makes me better.

US

Oh, we play,
But this love's not a game,
We put all our effort into it,
It's well maintained.
We're on the same level,
Connected soul, heart and brain.
The addition of this happiness
Has been the subtraction of pain.
A relationship that's a picture of perfection,
We fit in that frame.
The love of my lady, I state my claim,
And in it, I devote my faith.
In the arms of an angel,
There's no better place
And a kiss from her lips,
There's no better taste.

Perfection

If she's not perfect,

Then ten's the wrong measurement,

For perfection has to be heaven sent.

She's an angel from every angle;

God put work in to create this Queen's beginning.

A blessing to me, she perfectly chose my life to fit in,

And she's been just the right size.

There's no better picture that has been painted

Or song that has been sung more beautiful than her in my eyes.

To hold her is to grasp the colors of a rainbow

Or to hug a spring wind as it blows.

Man, I love this woman,

And I let it show

Because, Lord knows she's the essence of perfection

From the top of her head to her pedicured toes.

I Want

Time has revealed some things that I was feeling.
I've been so sick of loneliness,
And the cure is much more than her sexual healing.
It's funny how time can define
That which you can't find the meaning
And bring to light what's directly in your sight.
Yet, you really haven't been seeing.
Do we really need love to be pushed or shoved all in our face
In order to taste or be wrapped in its embrace?
I'm tired of the wait
So ready for the one sent from heaven to be my mate
A part of my fate.
Time changes days and dates, but it also reveals what is real,
And it's brought my dream into my reality
And given me something to feel.

I'm Spinning

I've been celebrated for painting beautiful pictures through my words,

But if you dig deep down inside of me,

My inspiration goes no further than her.

My foundation be she,

For she inspires me to be all that I can be.

I'm a movement on my own,

But she's a major part of the motivation in me.

My dreams have become my realities,

For she has made them something to see.

I've found that love without limits,

And I'm so blessed to be in it.

I've got a Queen on my team,

And we've shared our winnings, since our beginnings.

No matter how you spin it, our future together is bright,

And I'll always write stories with the happiest endings.

Attention

Today as men, we celebrate our foundation, the Queen.

By all means, you are greatness seen and heard,

Beauty by sight and knowledge through word.

To disrespect you is absurd,

For you are the reason we as men do most of what we do;

It's for the love of you.

You deserve the praise, 365 days,

Yet we celebrate two.

You're more than a mother and a woman; you are the glue,

And this is to express our love for you.

You are appreciated by me and many men,

You are our beginning and where we want to be in the end.

I salute you, Queens,

Our homie, our lovers,

And most of all, our very best friends.

A Borrowed Snatch

I'll be her comforter as long as she's yours.

I'm wanting her as long as she's willing to leave out my back door.

I'm fronting for her.

I'll give her everything that you don't.

I'm all the wills that you won't.

When you leave her alone, I'm on the phone,

While you're playing the dog, she's play with my bone,

Then, I can send her ass home, because I want to be alone.

You're relationship problems, I don't got them.

When I wants that ass, I text her ass

And just hits send,

And we're fuckin' again and again.

Trust me, your ass is just on lend,

I don't want to be her man; I'm just her fuckin' friend.

Then, when she gets emotionally attached,

I'll find a new snatch, and you can have yours back

Because that's the beginning of the end.

I'm Not Your Bitch.Com

A bad bitch will shit on the floor,

Chew on your shoes, and walks on all fours.

When she's out that door, for sure she's a slut,

Any dog can fuck, even the mutts.

With tail in the air, her breed ain't rare,

When that pussy's in heat, any cat can beat.

Believe me, if you're a lady, you're never a bitch,

Not a good one or bad one, not even the greatest.

Don't open doors for others to say this, because if you say it,

Those haters will play with it,

And unless you're walking on all fours

And shitting on floors

You ain't no bitch.

That Good Shit

That good love;

The kind you crave on lonely days;

When she walks in that door, you're simply amazed.

Good love;

It puts your sanity on the shelf and makes you crazy.

The kind of love

That has you calling a grown muthaf**ka, baby.

It keeps you wanting that time,

All the time,

And any time,

Anywhere,

And everywhere.

That good love

That will have you sharing sh*t

That you're normally selfish with.

Love that's too legit to quit,

And you damn sure ain't parting with.

Love that will make a peaceful man shoot a dude

And a lady stab a bi**h all in their shit.....

That Good Fit

Oh, when she was made,

It had to be a sunny day,

Rain had no place,

Storms had to find a new space.

She's as bright as the sun rays

But as comfortable as a spot in the shade.

This woman is the main ingredient in how you make love.

The beauty of her heart, mind, soul all of the above.

Who she is fits me to a tee and hugs me like gloves.

All those who's are once was,

There's no doubt about it; she gets all this love.

Affection is thrown in her direction, emotionally,

Physically, her hearts under my protection.

No divisions or subtractions;

I've added multiple levels of satisfaction

To make this thing happen.

Shhhhhhh...

I wrote a whisper for her ear,
And its destination was her heart.
My intentions are always affectionate;
As her man, I plays my part.

I've been about good loving from the start,
And there's no ending in sight.
I've made loving this woman constantly
My one and only plight.

I so love her life,
And that's not just because she put me in it.
She gave her tender heart to me,
And I was more than willing to win it.

I've been living for more than a minute,
But she made new every breath I take,
So, it feels like my life's just beginning.
My God has placed an angel in my life,
And now, heaven is my ceiling.

Gone

Words don't work, anymore.
Love has began to take steps toward an open door,
It's gone!!

That which was beautiful music
Has become such a sad song.
She's still here, but she's gone.

Gone are the times when I could make her smile
Just by being in her presence.
Now, our moments just seem irrelevant.

It's evident that I still love this Queen,
But gone is the dreams of happily ever after,
And that's my reality.

Can I get back that which has gone?
Can I make it strong, again
By just rekindling a friendship, first?

The words don't work,
But I'm willing to work
As hard as it takes to retake the love that has gone.

My Match

I've had what I thought was love

That held me down and held me back.

Now, I've found love

That holds me down and has my back.

And it's like that;

I gives it right back.

True love is about building,

And I've got stacks on top of stacks.

I'm emotionally attached to my perfect match;

Loneliness had to take a back seat to compatibility.

It's all about my baby,

Because she makes it all about me,

And that's what's up.

All those who may oppose what we got,

We ain't giving a fuck.

This thing here that we share is a blessing,

Not a hoping,

Or a wishing,

Or just mere luck.

My Perfect Fit

I write with the insight and the fight for love.
I'm looking for that lady that fits me like a glove;
Pure love the vision of doves;
Minus the shit that birds come with.
If I wanted to deal with shit, I'd be dating toilets.

I prefer that lady that will take my heart
And spoil it by keeping it warm and adoring it.
Take this love from my core
And cherish it by storing it.

Let me be the man that she wants,
And she'll be my unbelievable miss,
And we'll cosign each day
With a signature kiss.

Happiness

Her window of opportunity has closed;

I left her loneliness out in the cold.

I mated her soul and gave her something to hold on to,

Someone to believe in.

We have dreams of achievement;

I've become someone to team with.

She's a God's gift to my present and has blessed my future.

I address all her needs, so I'm exactly what suits her.

All the he's, hims and thems are simply a blurr.

I'm the main ingredient of the main course; happiness to occur.....

I ain't felt unhappiness, since I've found my happiness,

Queen she is now, for she used to be a princess.

Good's what I used to be, 'til I've attached myself to greatness.

The anticipation of a partner in crime is done,

Because the time has come,

For this dude has found his one.

Love is fun when it's associated with amazing in the form of a woman.

What a blessed man I am, for she stands by my side;

A lady all day, but yet, she's my ride or die.

Yes, I can state with pride,

Her being a hell of a chick makes me one hell of a guy.

Touched By An Angel

Have you ever been touched
By an angel on your private parts?
Your mind, your soul,
Did she caress your heart?

Have you been held by the wings
Of a woman so beautifully amazing,
That you would give her your all
And your everything?

Does time stand still
When you're in the thrill of her presence?
Are you hooked by her words
And punctuated in her sentence?

Not to mention, the glow of her essence
Had an unfocused man paying attention.
God's greatest invention, I request permission to hold.
Has an angel ever touched your heart, mind, body and soul?

My Vision

Once her feelings were revealed,
My feelings got real.
She's personifies beauty throughout her whole being;
Not just with sex appeal.
She's that sweet touch of love,
Giving me something to feel.

My proposal
Is at her disposal,
That's without the kneel
Or before the ring.

I profess that she's the best part of my everythings.
Anywhere she's at is where I want to be.
She's a vision of happiness, and it's what I want to see
Focused is me when she's my 20/20.
So rich am I,
Her worth is infinite money.

My Support

Yes, I love her,

So I hug her with words

Before I place my arms around her physical.

My feelings are off life support;

Emotions are no longer critical.

There's no I in our team,

But we're so in step that we move like an individual.

My principle

Is that she's the principal in my school of thought.

I can't be derailed;

She keeps my mind on track;

She's the focus on my train of thought.

I found my right one after all sorts of wrongs,

For I was once weak, and she made me strong.

In the presence of my Queen,

My loneliness is absent and long gone.

She's the lines of a poem and the words to a song.

Ain't nobody got shit on her,

Not even King Kong.

One Of A Kind

It would be simply asinine to define her by her fine,

But then again, she's a ten because of her beautiful mind.

A one of a kind masterpiece by God's own design,

And then, he broke the mold.

She's a Queen if eyes have ever seen one, truth be told.

I'd give a piece of my soul to hold her,

For that is as rare as grabbing a snow flake out of mid-air

And possessing it.

It's like God put her in my life for the sake of my heart

And blessing it.

And she's been caressing it, ever since.

My stories of a lonely man

Are now written in script and in past tense.

My feelings are relevant to my ladies amazing elegance.

Happy is this man to be in the presence of an angel;

A circumference of love from all angles.

She untangled and unraveled my feelings;

Put my love under new management.

I believe that she was conceived

But Lord knows, she was heaven sent.

My Seed

She's oh so much more

Than the allure of what you see,

But she's all that I adore;

You can see that by looking at me.

I've got this glow in my eyes

When she's by my side,

Her natural beauty

Makes my nature rise.

She be the seed that makes my love tree grow,

Every leaf is a sign that lets me know.

God don't make mistakes,

And he took his time to create a woman who's great.

With the strength of an ocean,

Deep as the sea,

The flow of a river,

But as steady as a lake.

I'll give all that she can take.

She holds me down, so I can carry our weight,

But wait; with this kind of miss, then happiness is my fate.

The One

She is, was, and always will be the love of my life.
A princess at birth;
A Queen through her life.
So significant I pray
That I can make her my magnificent other.
Her worth is measured by so much more
Than how good of a lover she is.
She's class personified.
High class is how she lives.
No expectations of reparations
For all that she gives.
I have admiration for a lady
Who's a hell of a woman.
A handler and manager of any situation,
With a loving heart without hesitation.
This woman's all you could want,
Up front and has your back,
There's nothing that she lacks.
She's all that and then some,
She's one in a million; yes, she's the one.

The Friendly Ghost

The friendship boat sails,
Even when the family boat won't float.
True friendship is a comforter
When blood will leave you soaked.
A best friend is an extension of your best hand.
A good friend is your best man or a hell of a woman.
By your side no matter the situation that you're put in.
By your side during your losses,
As well as celebrating the wins.
A dear friend will wipe your tears
Before they have time to reach your chin.
He'll tell you she's no good,
Or she'll let you know to stop fuckin' with him.
A great friend is by your side
When shit gets thick; even when shit is thin.
If that's your dog, homie,
If she's ya gurl,
Then, you're friends 'til the end.

The Sign

When love don't live there, anymore,

Doors don't get slammed; they get quietly closed.

When love has gotten up and gone,

You won't notice the bags or the missing clothes.

Before love makes its exit,

There's something that shows there's something you know.

Love just doesn't just get up and go,

There's been signs of a storm; not just a simple wind blow.

When you've been living in sunshine,

You must notice the clouds.

Love just don't get up and leave you

Wondering what's this all about.

Love may slip away,

But not without something to say.

When love's had enough,

You can't beg it to stay.

My Love

Oh, she's got my world

In the palm of her hands.

She's a hell of a woman,

Which makes me a hell of a man.

I extend myself to be all that I can.

I'm a movement for self,

But I'm even greater when by my side she stands.

I'm a success,

Because she's the main ingredient in all of my plans.

If I'm a million dollar man,

I'm worth much more with the one that I adore;

An angel without wings, mi amigo mi amore.

Forever Valentine

When all the chocolates gone
And the flowers have dried up and died…

Is the expression of love still there?
Is the love still alive?

365, come along for the ride!
My love is a marathon; never a sprint.

You won't have to wait 364 days
To see where love went.

Love has no limits; it's not measured with dollars and cents
Or displayed for a day that just came and went.

It's about moments in time
Spending; not how much was spent,
Love is 365, ladies and gents.

My Everyday Rose

I have no poems to write
Or sweet words to say, today,
For she has my heart each and every day.
365 I'm alive, because she's by my side,
Not just February 14th 365 you can't divide.
365 you can't hide behind flowers
And candy in a heart shaped box.
365 means I love you a lot,
My loves non-stop.
It's well displayed everyday in everyway
Without the use of manmade props.
365 I gives all I've got from January 1st to December 31st
I puts my love on top.
Roses are red, and violets are blue
But 365 days are the days that I celebrate my love for you.

Sex On A Platter

Oh, I'm nasty!
She tried to slip that ass pass me,
But I've got x-rated vision
With x-ray precision.
I can make an assurance
That my dick and her pussy will have a collision.
I placed my instrument
In her incision;
This is fuckin' livin'.
She likes taking it, and I'm willing;
Giving 'cuz I'm a giver.
When my dick's UPS, I deliver,
Her lips quaver all of them.
She keeps her legs open
With anticipation of my cum, again.
She appreciates my services,
And she serves me on a platter.
Bedroom, living room,
The kitchen counter,
It doesn't matter.

Burn Out

I puts my skill set on deck,

Yes, I plays my hand.

Oh yeah, I masturbates,

But my dicks in her hand

And then in her mouth.

She sucks that which she didn't jerk out,

I've got her stretched out for a JPB workout.

I gets her burned out, leg lifts, ass splits.

She don't wanna play no more she can't cum out.

The pussy's happy, but the lips pout.

I hit it with different strokes.

I fill lips with my Mr. Drummond Willis

What you talkin' bout.

She wants a rerun with my Rodger

Hey, hey, hey it's no bother.

Hands smackin' it ass clappin'

Shit now that's what's happening!!

Always A Lady

The beauty of your titties
And ass will pass,
But it's your ability to maintain class
That's gonna last.
Over exposure can turn over
And have them treat you like trash.
If the first thing I notice is ass crack or cleavage,
I'm gonna wanna smash.

That's temporary lust;
Not an investment but fast cash.
Then you want to know why your ass is stashed,
Because what I saw in you relationships aren't built,
Do the math.
I'm out the door when your bottom hits bottom
And the titties sag.
It may not be funny
But you've got to laugh
When you're sittin' with a fifth
A hand lookin' at the pics of what you use to have.

I Fly

I don't get high,
But I fly on the wings of an angel.
She completes my circle
With love from every angle.
We never get it twisted,
But our feelings have become tangled.
No missing our decision
To make single a thing of the past.
We've become tight like glue;
We want love to last.
Our foundation is laid;
She gives me the warmth of sunshine
And I provides her with the comfort of shade.
I know my woman's worth, and I stay paid,
They say love is a house,
And that's how our mansion was made.

Best Side of Me

All that I've got she gets.

She keeps my love light lit, and I'm not blowing it.

She's my best thing going, and I know it.

My feelings are displayed,

Not just by saying but by showing,

And I'm a poet.

I can paint a picture of love unconditional

In some lines I wrote, title it a love note.

I quotes myself with my actions.

I can say it pretty well,

But my reactions are her satisfaction.

The words formed an attraction,

But my movements are what made it happen.

Now we've got love and happiness,

Not from wishes or luck,

but because we are blessed.

Everlasting Impression

Oow my baby fine!

A dime?

Try multiplying that 1000 times.

Beauty in abundance she shines,

She's a sun kiss on a horizon.

There couldn't be a picture painted or lyrics written

To have a man smitten more than she has me.

Where she's at is where I want to be.

I'm a King because she's a Queen,

She makes my realities feel like dreams.

No one comes before or after nor in between,

We are the team

and our winning has been since our beginnings.

Happiness with no view of endings

just this love we share consistent and continuing.

Nursery Rhyme

Peter Piper picked off a pair of pretty panties.

Peter Piper put his pipe in her pink pussy.

Peter Piper has a fixation and fascination with fulfilling freaky fantasies.

Peter Piper fancies fuckin' while fondling fat asses.

If Peter Piper is placed in a room with pink pussy with no pink panties

then Peter Piper is fuckin' smashin'!!!

Roll Of The Die

She put her cookies in the hands of a monster,

And I ate her up.

The way I eats the pussy

Is the prelude to a fuck.

She goes koo koo for multiple nuts.

She likes cummin' and stuff.

She gets one from the tongue,

But that ain't enough.

Oh, so tender,

But she craves it rough,

She likes making love,

But she loves to fuck.

I placed three kisses on her wish list,

And she gives me luck.

Ride On The Wild Side

I slides right in,

Like hard bottoms on hockey floors.

She keeps her legs closed,

But for me she's got revolving doors.

Game smooth like lead singer of the Commodores.

I make pussy wet like sea shores.

Brand new panties become disposable draws.

She puts that ass in my paws,

When she's on all fours.

We be steady rockin' baby no time to pause.

I put a clause in her contract, so I works for that.

I hits from the back to side on top and back again

And she's throwin' right back.

Ain't no slackin' in what we packin'.

We make 100% cotton sheets feel like satin.

Now that's what's happening!!!!

Love Lines

Be My Boss

I peel her panties off
As if I'm slidin' dental floss.
I pays the pussy sooo much attention,
She calls me her punanny boss.
Forever in her split,
I lick it until I comes up hoarse.
I sucks titties and smacks ass,
But my desires in the main course.
No delay with my tongue play
I hits her main source.
No problem for me gettin' to her core,
The pussy attorney at law,
I counsel her pussy and panty divorce.
She likes it rough in her,
So soft my stimulation got her navigation turned off
It's got the man in the boat so lost.

While You Were Sleeping

Yes, he's your man,
So treat him so.
You can't belittle a brother
And expect a relationship to grow.
If you plant seeds of hate
That's you relationships fate.
Yeah chick talk behind his back
But be in your man's face
Because they see and hear how you talk to him
And would gladly take your place.
While you're high on your cloud
Their looking to replace,
Walk in your shoes
Sleep in your space.
Yes, these sistas crave the taste of your mate.
You got what they pray for, for heaven sake.
A good man is right in your face,
But keep treating him how you do,
And he'll be gone faster than you can be fake.

Forever My Friend

I'm smart enough to know that she chose me.

I just put myself in position to be chosen.

Ever since then, she's been the best thing I've got going

And I'm showing that she is my truth and I'm knowing.

My shine comes from her glowing.

We don't skip a beat we're steady flowing.

Love so deep we're an ocean of devotion.

I'm consumed with love.

She's my love potion number 9 and 10.

I mean these feelings are infinite.

Yes, I love my best friend.

Look And You Shall Find

She's my best friend and confidant.
She's been who I've wanted and remains all that I want.
She was told this up front,
She was showed this up front.
My feelings are the truth she knows I'm no front.
We've been searching for love,
And we've put an end to our hunt.
My baby, my lady amazes me just being who she be,
And I know that I've been blessed by her being with me.

.

The Champ

My mind frame is Django unchained.

When the D is silent, my offense is a challenge.

To the mentally challenged, I'm too much to be challenged.

Their incapable of challenging this word play King.

I won't say I'm amazing, but my word play's astonishing.

I've won the belt, the trophy, and the muthafuckin' ring.

Before the bell rings or the Oh say can you see

My challengers have dismissed all possibilities of victory.

The losses are viewed as acceptable,

And 2nd place has become a type of collectable.

Mentally, I'm meat and potatoes,

And these dudes are just plain vegetables.

Mental vegetarians, and I'm a 3 course meal.

I'm the Greatest, Iron Mike, Money May and the Real Deal.

Two For One

I'm a pussy wetter
Like a pussy sweater
In humid weather.
Me and pussy go together
Like crackers and cheddar.
I makes the pussy feel better.
She calls me cat nip.
I fucks her with Richard;
She gets all of the dick,
Not just the tip.
She's ti of tiny,
Her boy comes equipped.
She's amazed by my fuckin'
I guess she's miracle whipped.
I've won gold for my x game
With a move called smashDpussyNspilt.

Love Is Blind

The moment she leaves my sight,

My focus is lost.

The value of what she means to me,

Lord knows there is no cost.

This love we've got,

We ride like ross.

Relationship equality,

There is no boss.

Sex filled with spice,

We needs no sauce.

Physical attraction

Before clothes come off.

Love's not a sickness,

There is no cough.

We work our way through the rough times

With feelings so soft.

We've been winning

From our beginnings;

We've never experienced loss.

Forever Beauty

Sisters, let no miss nor mister dismiss
The beauty you know exists.
It may seem harsh to say this,
But give them your beautiful ass to kiss.
Your wonders in life won't consist
Of things that they have on their wish list.
Be who you are, not what they insist you to be.
You've got to be the best of you,
Not them, nor me.
Your beauty comes from your possibilities,
Not their insecurities.
Beauty is more than skin deep;
It's seen through knowledge of self respect
For others and how you represent
Yourself physically and verbally.

It's What We Do

What me and Boo do is called fuckin'.
I'm pussy lickin', she's dick suckin',
I beats the pussy up while she's ass buckin'.
Bed wettin' from fuckin' sweatin'.
Profane slang bitches niggas with no regretin'.
Cum runnin', and I'm catchin'.
It's a hell of a beatin' I'm givin' to her midsection.
My weapon of choice is an erection;
Felony assault, she put the pussy into witness protection.
No order for protection, we likes it raw.
I dogs the pussy out when she's on all fours.
I started in her front, but I finished back door.
No love makin' tunes, we Fucks hardcore.

Dissolving Heart

Baby come back to me.

A heart that was so full of you is now running on empty.

These feelings I'm having they tempt me to pick up the phone,

But the fear of your voice saying leave me alone

Is a tone I couldn't bear to hear.

I'm a brave man,

But the fear that you won't be there

Has my brown eyes filling with tears.

I've imagined the years we'd spend loving one another.

The true friendship we have, not to mention

The loving, kissing and hugging.

The absence of you in my life has got this man straight bugging.

So baby, come back to me;

I promise I'll change.

This hurts too deep for a band aid;

Only you can take away my pain.

Mistletoe

On top of my Christmas wish list was a kiss,
But I've been a naughty boy so my chimey, Santa, chose to skip.
No quality time under the mistletoe with that beautiful miss.
There's no gift you can replace that with.
The anticipation had a grown man feeling like a toys R us kid.

Sorrys don't matter when you did what I did.
'Tis the season to be giving, and I've got this love to give,
But I want to receive.

Oh, I want to believe that she's still loving me,
But it's hard to see what's not under my Christmas tree.
No french hens or turtle doves;
I want french kisses and good love.
No lights, no bulbs, just the glimmer of her eyes
And the comfort of her hugs.

Sunset Over Love

Without her, I'm simply a man alone,

Left to deal with his mistakes.

She gave her love to me, and for granted I did take.

Something so beautifully precious,

I didn't hesitate to break.

Now, these tears I make

Are a product of the fate I made.

How did I destroy the house

Even before the foundation was laid.

Now, this clouds hanging over me;

I blew off sunshine for this spot in the shade.

A Queen is she, and a King I was made.

I realize that I fucked up on love in so many ways.

If I had one more chance, I'd humbly say:

I love you,

And you are the best thing that's happened to me in quit a long time.

You had no clue,

But I've prayed that you would be mines.

I've written lines full of love with you on my mind.

My love for you is anyway, everyday,

In every way, and all the time.

Play Your Rule

She said, 'I was wifey when you liked me.
Muthafucka, if you love me like you say you do,
Then you gotta fuckin' wife me.
Get dirt on that knee, muthafucka, and for life me,
Or get a front row seat to watch me leave.
If you've truly got love for me,
Don't just say it, let me see or let me be.
Make me a fact of your life;
I won't be just relationship curiosity.'

Smoke Break

I've got her makin' love faces in inappropriate places.

Knees rubbin' together nipples all hard at her work station.

Thong needs drying 'cuz it's filled with liquidation.

Anticipation makes her hate waitin'

For quittin' time and the walk to the train station.

Her fascination with my verbalization

Makes her take smoke breaks for masturbation;

And she don't even smoke.

She's in the ladies room on full stoke

With the man in boat.

She don't miss a note

French tips got fully dipped with a cum coat.

Transform Me

I had a dream of a Queen who made me her King.

It was absolutely amazing;

She gave me everything,

And I gave it back.

It was proof positive of where my heart was at.

The love that she shared with me was more than enough.

It was the most valued gift; not all the material stuff.

Those shine things meant nothing to me.

For in the arms of The Queen is where I wanted to be.

To be with she, you can take the kingdom from me.

With a love this strong, royal will be all our possibilities.

GM I dream about words!!!!!

I Just Knew

The first time I held her in my hands,

I knew I wouldn't let her go.

Not much curiosity about this love;

It's something I just know.

Me and her just flow, and it feels so good.

I came into her life and stole her heart; a relationship robin hood.

A fairytale in the shape of female.

A Queen to me; it's so clear to me, she contains every detail.

Others fail in comparison.

God broke the mold, so she's the only one.

She's a homie, a lover, a friend;

She's made my lonely done.

Let Me Mend You

I picked up every piece of her broken heart,
So, I gave her reason to believe.
Her heart had been torn apart;
I became the glue that she needs.
She sees the grass is green
After pulling all those weeds.
She wants a tree with foundation;
She's tired of having to keep planting seeds.
An angel wants to fly, again,
And I mended her wings.
Experiences in the negative,
She deserves some positive things.
She gets all the love I've got for my Queen;
I'll do anything.
I'll go anywhere at any time.
She knows I'll cradle her heart,
Because she made it mines.

What We Do

She simplifies love, because loving her is easy.

She doesn't do anything extraordinary;

Just being herself is what pleases me.

To the 10th degree I've got belief in we.

With the love that we've got, all things are possibilities.

My foundation, my stability,

A love so strong.

We flip the script;

We've got relationship agility.

Late Night Snack

I visits her bodega, frequently.
She keeps her legs open 24 hours for me.
The power of the pussy got me spending dividends.
I'm a shopaholic, and she thanks me for her cum, again.
My credits good with her, so she lets me cum, again.
I'm shoppin' light; she's got no bags for the pipe,
So, she feels me cummin' in.

Position

Sistas, the hands of a good man
Won't leave imprints on your skin.
The words from his mouth
Don't tear you down from within.
Your beautiful smiles
Won't be reduced to insecure grins.
He'll be your teammate;
By your side to comfort you during losses
And to celebrate your wins.
You're a woman to the world
But a Queen to him.
He shows exactly what you mean to him.
No one comes in between you and him.
He'll stay true to you,
Even if it means he can't fuck with them.

God's Watch

My Timeline is by God's design.
You can act shady if you want;
I'll be walking on sunshine.
I stepped on cloud 9, skipped 10 to 11.
Heaven sent, so on my way back to that which I went
But got some repentin' to do.
Lord knows I'm an unfinished masterpiece,
And he's far from through with me.
I stay true to him, 'cuz ain't no fooling him.
My timeline is by God's design
From my beginning to my end.

Fallen Angel

I grabbed the wing of an Angel

And wrapped her up in my arms.

I had desires to be her comforter

And keep her safe and warm.

I promised to be her calm before the storm

And her sunshine when it's gone.

I've been her happiness after she's been love scorned.

No longer love torn, our love is one, and it's new born.

She's been turned off of love,

But we got hooked up, and that power's back on.

Now, we're living a song.

I grabbed the wing of an Angel,

And in my arms, she belongs.

Stand Up And Represent

I've laid down the blueprint for insensitive gents.

If you make some addition to the love you claim,

You can subtract some of her vents.

If she's your heaven sent,

When she's out of eye sight, she still represents.

Cherish the moments or be remembering where they went.

Keep it 100 all the time;

She's worth much more than your 50 cents.

The good man at her side must stand,

Because to her that's the shit that makes sense.

Written In Stone

They say no one is perfect, but she's as close as it gets.

She's always on my mind; no need for retrospect.

She's my puzzle piece; we perfectly connect.

She gets all that I've got, 'til I've got nothing left.

I'll love her 'til it's my last breath.

You know that means I love her to death.

That's my word, and it's set in stone.

She maintains her position as my focal point,

Even when I'm alone.

Love, no limits; my affection's full blown.

I still can feel her touch

And smell her sweet, even when she's long gone.

I can't hold a note, but I can drop a song.

You are everything, and everything is you.

Come and Share my life,

'Cuz All I want is you.

Love Heal Me

I'm not a fairy tale,

She believes in me.

My actions speak louder than words;

I give her something to see.

She's my doctor love;

She brings out the best of me.

Love surgery; she must specialize in hearts.

For she's been an intricate part of repairing mines.

Love and happiness in my future,

She's the warning sign.

I'll do all I can to keep her mines.

Love, protection and affection all the time.

I'm happy to bask in the warmth of her everyday shine.

With Come A Dream

Pleasing her is a purpose for me.

Making her happy;

I acknowledge I do it purposefully.

I'm King to her Queen.

I go all out; I'm in full support of her team.

On two feet, she's a dream; pleasure for her by any means.

Truth be told, never need to come clean.

She's all I ever want; I'm her fiend.

Never Forgotten

How silly of me

That it would neglect my she.

No, not me;

I'm disciplined; for her I will be all I can be.

I'll do all I can to be all that she needs.

Her love is times 3.

She's become an addition to me.

Love may blind for some, but she is my focus,

And that's so clear to see.

My affections 20/20.

Her wealth's beyond any amounts of money.

I'm willing to share this life,

So, there's not a damn thing she can't get from me.

Angel In Disguise

There are many things that I have to be thankful for;
Life, good health, the love of family and friends.
Recently, a good friend has come back into my life
And has become motivation and inspiration,
And I am truly thankful.
There may not be a handful of people in your life
That have enough love for you to want better for you
Without the thoughts of any gains for themselves.
God has placed angels on earth in human form.
And I am blessed to have an angel as a friend.

Locked Heart

Yeah. I love her

And she knows it 'cuz I shows it.

My actions speak louder than any words;

I do more than propose it.

I values her worth enough not to blow this

With the body of a man and the mind of a kid.

I don't devalue her feelings; I know how important this is.

I thank God for this love that she so willingly gives.

She'll know that my love is true;

It'll be shown full blown as long as I live.

'Til death do us part.

My love is a house, and she's got the key to my heart.

Lunch Break

I put in hard work underneath her skirt with my dickie.

I asked for overtime; she had me scheduled for a quickie.

All the cum she released made the situation sticky.

She shouted on a down stroke how she wasn't fuckin' wit me,

But I ignored it, of course.

I stuck my tongue in her main course,

And she fucked me with her oral intercourse.

She takes me in with a slight cough.

We do it so hard that we're both hoarse.

Our Kinda Love

I want that Presidential love,
Michelle and Barack.
I've had that ghetto shit,
That Love and Hip-Hop.
I want the view from the top.
That good love 'til the last drop,
It keeps me craving her amore.
Eyes get wide open
When she walks through the door.
When the loves all that it keeps,
You wanting it more and more
Affection galore.
Just the taste of her kisses
Makes me want an encore.

You And I

I write these words
As a token of my affection.
My words, so empowering,
To deepen this connection.
They seem that strong,
Because they're arms for your protection.
Not to mention,
They send love in your direction,
And you mean so much.
It's hard to play tough
When you miss a tender touch.
These words are of love, not lust.
These words aren't about me, or you,
They are about us.

My Inspiration

I've been inspired by scholars
To be addicted to knowledge, not the dollar.
Lead by example,
And you will be looked at to follow.
Maintain your own;
Don't loan and don't borrow.
Happiness will acknowledge your life.
No comprehension of pain, nor of sorrow.
Every day is a blessing,
So you look forward to tomorrow.
Let love fill up your heart,
And your life won't seem hollow.

My Sweetness

I nicknamed my lady Sugarface,

But she's absolute sweetness in every place.

Every taste of her is candy coated.

My love for her is truthfully noted.

No doubt about, it I'm truly devoted,

And she knows it.

My whispers in her ears are spoken in the tone of a poet,

And they sound like verses to a love song.

She's got the sexiness of a thong with all her clothes on.

She is my all right in those moments that seem all wrong.

Her beauty equal to her strong.

My baby be my dominant hand; she's my right arm.

This I swear, I'm gonna love her 'til I'm gone.

I loves my Sugarface to death with feelings that are still newborn.

I Changed Her

She must have fell from heaven,

Right into my arms

And ever since that moment,

She's been turning me on.

With the beauty of a Luther song,

She's a masterpiece.

She just added one to my life,

But how it made my love increase.

Such a treat delicious from head to feet.

Sex appeal undeniable all around just sweet.

She love her he, and I loves my she,

And us, together, is an incredible we!!!!

Well Damn

I love making fuck,

And she fuckin' loves makin' me happy.

Her ass tends to totally agree the way that it be clappin'.

No panties on, she makes so easy for unwrappin'.

I fuck her 'til she's blackin' out.

She can't remember how all that happened.

My Love

No yo llamado Miguel,
But all I want is you to do is let this love Adorn Boo.
Baby, come and share this life.
I know that's the title to a song, too,
But girl, I love you in a way that only poems can say.
My whispers in your ears sound like the songs they play.
You Are My Everything,
Always and Forever, you will be my Lady.
Beauty is Your Name; my sunshine after Candy Rain.
I know When a woman's fed up;
There's nothing you can do about it, but I intends no pain.

I Demand

I respects muthafuckas that respects me.

I checks muthafucks that X me.

I'm a gentleman, but I got the thug on deck.

A wordsmith, I create swords, so protect ya neck.

I keep flow in tow, so you know I catch wreck.

Stays zip lock fresh; so cold but stays hot

JPB is well kept.

The Star Player

I'm single, double, triple;
I cover all the bases.
I'm sunlight and brightness;
I shine on every place.
I'm a good look and a great smell;
I satisfy all your tastes.
I'm the NBA finals, World Series,
Super Bowl, and even the NASCAR chase.
Good, better, great.
I'm JPB, for heaven's sake.
I'm that good medicine;
I'm easy to take.

A Duplication

I'm copy and pasted.

I'm re-written and traced.

I'm a frown turned upside down.

I create happy faces.

I carries the mind to other places.

I'm just simply amazing.

Yes, I believe I'm the shit!!!!!

God's Creation

You were built by God to survive
The storm filled days and the darkest of nights.
You are made and prepared to face any plight.
You are a fighter in the war of life.
You can do and will do
You only settle for can't and might.
Never let your trials and tribulations
Make you lose sight.
This is your life; seize it, take control,
Because all that seems wrong will be alright,
For your creator is never wrong.
He is and forever will be all right!!!!

My Replacement

I've found a replacement,
OFFICAL!!!
She's all that, is her issue.
Sexy, smart; if beauty can be simple,
Then, she is simply beautiful.
A dream come true;
A Queen, through and through.
A heart so pure, it just requires your amore.
Easy to adore;
Class on deck with so much more in store.
She's something to look forward to
When on the other side of that door.
She's a detractor of the a,
Allure that other dudes crave for.
They can't walk in her shoes.
In an ugly ass world,
I've grabbed hold of something so beautiful.
Someone to be true to.
A lady, my baby, and dare I say, a Boo Boo.

My Support

I don't fall, because she's my kick stand.

I'm a better human being just being her man.

We go hand and hand;

She's the blue print to our plans.

My baby's the will to do when my thoughts say I can't.

She's my everything and my all the time.

A rainbow after the rain,

But every day, my sunshine and she's fine.

She be killin' em simply Fabulous.

She's my life with crime.

So, I write with rhymes for her.

I spends my time for us.

I treats her royally,

'Cuz she's a Queen, so it's a must.

Do Not Be Confused

Sexy don't get confused with low class hoes.

Sexy ain't caked up in Mac make up

Or have tramp stamped over the crack of her butt.

Sexy don't get confused with sluts.

Sexy doesn't look like she came out the house to get fucked.

Sexy be a lady all the time, no doubts, no maybe's.

Devalue herself; are you fuckin' crazy?

Sexy ain't a Gucci lady with a Nostrand Ave baby.

Sexy is a mom, not just a mother.

Sexy knows she's sexy with her titts and ass covered.

I Cater To The Ladies

My catering to the ladies feeds these dudes' hate.

It's not my fault their women are cummin' for me,

While they have to masturbate.

It starts with the words and ends in the shakes.

She's logged on in her cubicle;

To get home she can't wait.

She's got her panty liner on;

Pussy wet as a lake.

She anticipating pussy penetration

From a FB post.

Stimulation on this level was but a dream,

But I'm giving her hope.

I'm breaking all the rules;

I've got the man standing up in the boat.

When you're ghost,

She lets those fingers float

And you wonder why the sheet on your side of the bed

Is always soaked.

My Everlasting

My love for her is as deep as the sea,

And it's easy to see that without her,

I'm just a fish out of water.

When she's absent,

I crave the presence of her love and affection,

She gives my heart such an injection,

Life seems so right.

My Queen by all means,

She's my nights' moonlight and the beauty

And warmth of the sunrise, happiness to occur.

Empty

Heart still beating
It's still pumping blood, yet it's empty,
The sound of her voice,
Just for a moment seems oh so tempting.
This emptiness truly exists
And is absolutely worth mentioning,
But it's kept to myself.
Phone just inches away;
Thoughts of a call number still on display,
Area code dialed, then a delayed question to self:
What will I say?
I'm empty,
And nothing at this point for me is coming easy,
I'm missing the moments that we shared;
The ones that so please me.
Love level light is on;
Needle's on E.
I need to feel full, again, with that Super Woman incredible she.
Empty…
Is she thinking of me?
Is she also on empty without visions of me?
Is that a possibility
Or just the thoughts of a man running on empty?

His Son

I am a son of God;

My knowledge of this doesn't lead me to believe

That things won't be hard, at times.

He is the sun, the moon, and the stars;

Our Father who art in heaven, his love

Is giving me the ability to shine.

In his grace, I place all my faith,

Believing that his will be law

And he has never lost a case.

My pace has been set by the steps he allows me to make.

Those steps will consist of many mistakes,

Yet, I walk with faith.

With the Almighty to guide me,

I trust that I can see when my eyes are closed;

Heart open and my soul to give.

I don't pray, every day, but he knows this

And how much I appreciate the good, the bad,

The happy, and the sad of this life I live.

For I am a son Of God.

The Pursuit Of Happiness

Sirens blaring in the pursuit of happiness;
Red lights ran; stop signs ignored.
Adored is this feeling that you can't seem to catch up with.
You're speeding,
Getting side swiped and taking blind side hits.
Way past the limits set for self,
Worth has been put aside,
Because you've got your eyes on wealth.
Lane changing with your head light off,
No signals of thought,
Wheels keep turning, yearning to get happiness caught.
Breaking the laws of self respect and self esteem
For that ticket to ride in that dream.
To whip around in luxury's lap has got you in a tailspin;
No assurance, yet you keep taking collisions to your front end.
There seems to be no means to an end.
Happiness seems to have told you no parking, again,
So, your pursuit gets no brakes.
Full throttle; foot to the floor.
The allure has given you no choice but to accelerate,
No road blocking happiness,
For it is your dead end;
Your fate.

That Cougar

She said she's a cougar;

More like a saber tooth tiger.

55 years old;

More like in 55, she retired.

Black and white drivers license, class H,

She can operate a horse and Carriage.

Married to a slave her first marriage,

Taking a shit in the house was considered living lavish.

Southern bell picked cotton in the Carolina's old school country,

Don't believe in shaving the vagina,

Gray hairs everywhere down there.

Looks good for her age, hour glass shape,

An ass like a pear,

Not a care in the world,

Pension plan and Medicare.

She lies about her age;

Been 45 for at least 20 years.

My Reason For Being

There's not a star that graces a sky,
Nor a flower or sunrise
More beautiful than what I see in you.
You are all that a man could want in his life;
Motivation for an imagination to do what it do;
A dream come true, through and through;
The detail of a fantasy the clue to love's mysteries;
Reason to believe that there exist an Almighty;
Another you is not likely.
The essence of your presence more than excites me,
The opening of a heart so pure with open arms, it invites me.
I must confess that my poetical prowess
Would be much less without your highness as my topic.
You add to my love for words,
And there's just no way to stop it.

Queen

You have been brought to this earth

To have royal as your worth,

From birth, a Queen in the making.

Princess was but your first step, and you've kept on stepping.

A Queen's place is to sit upon her throne;

I guess you left yours in heaven.

Beautiful leader of the pack at that,

God must have used both hands in your creation

There will never be your match.

Little girls look up to you, grown women stand in admiration,

Your presence is always evident, your life's a special occasion.

Queen which is pictured in a man's dreams,

Class personified, an angel minus the wings,

Yet simply amazing.

Poetry in motion, a sunrise cascading the horizon

The moonlight kissing the sky,

Soul as deep as the ocean.

Any notion that you are not absolute perfection

Is a misdirection of sensible thought,

Queen, you are the reason kingdoms have been lost

And wars have been fought.

She Is My Portrait

I traced her tatt with my tongue,
Added all the colors, every one.
I redesigned that which was done so fine,
Every corner got hit, all lines well defined.
Like Pacasso, I painted her silhouette;
This kind of canvas isn't easy to get.
I've gained access to her assets;
Her private artist, I've traced her tatt,
In the darkest of rooms, my tongue knows exactly where it's at.
Drawn to draw out her pleasurable moments,
Kisses placed gently on all her components.
Not an inch shall I omit;
Your body picture painted with my lips with well placed kisses.
Let me dip into your ink well and bite what you like;
God made you a work of art, and oh what a sight you are.
Let my tongue trace that tatt;
I realize that's not where it's at,
But I want to mark all your body parts,
From your hairline to your heels.
Let me tattoo your tenderness with pleasure through pain
And make it look as good as it feels.

All A Man Needs

Pretty much,

She's pretty much a touch of class,

Her beautiful

Is beautiful without the display of ass.

With the worth that requires a calculator to add,

She's most valuable, I call her infinite math.

All that a man could want, she has,

Lord knows she would be a blessing to have.

Her blood type just might be P,

For her DNA is perfection to me,

And in her, it's perfection I see.

To explain is absolute simplicity.

On a scale of 1 to 10, she is 50 + 50

100% of heaven sent,

God places angels among us,

And her being makes this obviously evident.

My Dream

I have a dream that I would create speech with my pen.

My black history will be seen just as his story to all women and men.

My outreach will be to out reach all that is believed to be boundaries.

There will never be lines in my sand.

My plan is to ride life's waves to cross oceans

And crush the notion that any young black boy or girl's only success

Will be achieved through wishing and hoping.

Not only the athlete and rapper

From the street doors will be open or pole stroking,

Pray and belief in yourself will put great things in motion.

You are not and never were just a token,

You are a sky full of stars

With the strength to move mountains.

We were made to build, not just to climb.

My his story is to tell of my people,

Those not just of physical prowess,

But of our beautiful minds.

She Is

She is all that a man could want in his world,
Beautiful, a filler of emptiness, she has made my life full.
God answers prayers and it's crystal clear
That she is a blessing, exactly what's been missing.
Sometimes, a man needs the kind of affection
That comes from giving protection
To that special loved one.
I'm devoted to the notion
That her words aren't going to be sugar coated,
And she is that voice that I need to hear,
I want her here, for she is motivation
Injected in my ears.
My moments are hers to share;
I make moves to prove that I sincerely care.
She is no doubt reason
For a heart to be beating,
An R&B song through my wrongs
This Queen stands strong.
She is who I wish to have by my side for life's ride.
I spill out my insides with pride.
When things get off track I'm right back she is my guide,
Lights up my life.
She is amazing in more ways than I could ever mention,
For she is the focus of my greatest intentions.

My Steps Are Blessed

God gifted,

Blessed with a pen in my possession,

Uplifted,

Even though I fall short of living by the scripture.

Judge me not for you shall be judged.

Color me bad because I won't lie.

Black and white has never been my picture.

I've got faith and belief in the Almighty,

And though I've gone left sometimes,

I know that he guides me.

My path will be walked one step at a time,

And when it's my time, I'll go right, for he drives me.

The Journey Through Her Eyes

Her eyes, oh Lord;
Her eyes give the impression
Of the beauty you have intended for a tropical sunrise
Cascading over the gentle flow of the oceans waters.
The time you took to create her design
Must have taken a lot of sunrises and so much moonlight.
I'm put in such a state of happiness just at her sight.
All that could go wrong is gone,
Because of an angel you've placed in my life.
To say that all's right would be a slight untruth,
Because all is well with this fantasy female
Who has made disappear my relationship plight.
Lord knows you make no mistakes,
So this blessing of beautiful that you have blessed me with
I intend to intake.
Every bit of her, not one moment shall I waste,
Not the warmth of a hug or the taste of a kiss.

I Am Blessed

With the eyes of an eagle
Focused on success,
Goals written in gold
Steps to be the best.
Achievement seen in dreams,
Progression even at rest,
Standing on the mountain top,
Accepting nothing less.
God never promised an easy life,
So I humbly take my test,
They say that prayer changes things,
And it minimizes my stress.
I will maximize this mind of mines
And this thing beating in my chest.
Sometimes, doubts will arise in me,
I must confess.
I am convinced that I will commit
To the dedication and motivation of my prominence,
I don't crave fame, but still, the same,
I know that my name will be extremely relevant.

We Can Live Up To His Dream

I have a dream that I can live up to;
The dream that Dr. King believed for me.
We're living in a world that he had envisioned it to be,
Yet we still have room for growth.
We put more emphasis on designer clothes,
Alcohol consumption, and how much weed we smoke.
Education and participation in our community organizations
Is an absolute joke,
But is there hope, sometimes.
It seems so until you see our future
With their asses hanging out of their clothes.
Our kids killing our kids for who knows what;
We've got white supremacist
And members of the klan laughing at us.
Still, he had a dream of love and prosperity,
For the love of every man woman and child
To live together in unity.
Brothers and sisters of all colors and creeds;
Dr. King had a dream that we can still make our reality
If we only believe.

A Perfect Design

I would say she's the apple of my eye,

But that would be selling her short,

So I'll say she's my apple orchard.

If it takes a Queen to make a King complete,

Then my Queen is a major portion of my completion.

She gives me reason to believe in love unconditional;

She is my matter of fact.

To think that my life would be alright without her in it

Is simply fictional.

An absolute original angel,

Only God could design her kind of fine,

As sure as the sweetest grapes produce the finest wine.

She is the description of the definition of simply divine,

Truth be told, in every line I design,

With her on my mind.

They say that everyone has a twin, somewhere,

But me and the man upstairs knows

That this woman is one of a kind.

Being Humble

We tend to be strong
At doing what's wrong.
Our plight seems to be getting shit right.
Apology after apology is just sorry,
And that's not the person that we're trying to be;
Lord knows we can be better,
And who knows that better than we.

We should want to be more than what is said
And so much more than what is seen;
We don't want to be the line that causes division
Between us and a Queen.

A real man is a man who can humble himself;
Look within self and make adjustments his self,
Yet he's never too proud to reach out for help.
If you want your true wealth to equal her wealth,
Be a real man and put that pride on the shelf.

My Soft Voice

She's the eyes in back of my head,
My voice of reason,
My awareness of the things that I'm not seeing.
When doubt comes about, she's my believing.
Failure's not an option; she's my achievement.
God places people in your life with meaning,
And she's the definition of what I've been missing,
Her addition has subtracted my division
And multiplied good living.
Receiving her makes giving a blessing;
Happiness is an occurrence
When I'm blessed with her presence.
I've made it so evident that this woman,
This Queen to my life is so relevant.

My Inspiration

Lady in my life, I feel like a boy
With thoughts of his favorite toy on Christmas Eve night
Just from the sight of you.
It will be false to say that this love I have for you isn't true;
You are the inspiration and topic of my best material.
Simply fabulous, I'm so into you
I lust your mental and your physical.
This kind of love isn't original,
But it's spiritual.
Expression of my affection in your direction
Has become a ritual.

Just Convinced

Conceited?

Believe it.

Her mirror mirror on the wall lets her see it,

God outlined her fine to be it.

She speaks it;

Not in so many words but in a whole lot of actions,

Baby got those looks to die for;

Fatal attraction.

Style that brings smiles to even her haters,

Their tongues get twisted, so dissers turn into congratulaters.

Bad in so many good ways,

Gorgeous on display

With no pay,

While sistas got what she's got on layaway.

Eyes designed with felines in mind,

Lips made to kiss; aww s**t f*@k it,

She's that b*@ch.

The Strength Of A Woman

The strength of a woman doesn't come
From how many hours she spends in the gym,
And it damn sure don't come from the support of him.
Her power doesn't come from yoga or pilates,
Yet she's the essence of strength in so many ways.
The strength of a woman is gained and maintained
Through her walk, through trials and tribulations,
How the weight of the world rest on her back,
And she somehow holds on to her patience.
Her class is not graded on muscle mass or weights lifted,
Her bar isn't set by weight lifted
On a barbell at some weight station.
The strength of a woman pushes out 8 pounds of life
After 9 months of carrying it into its first vision of light.
Her plight is why writers write, why poets recite,
For her story must be told,
Lift her up for she's been held down while having to hold
It down by her damn self.
The strength of a woman is to value herself,
For no man needs stand and tell you that you are a Queen,
Priceless, and there's no limits to your wealth.

An Addiction

It can take years for you to find your Queen
And mere moments to lose her.
No more wishing for wishes for the wish you were.
Now, you're missing sleep over missing her.
The dreams that played in your slumber now are only a blur.
You start rewinding smiles from your memories of her.
It's no doubt about it, you're addicted to love.

Love Her My Way

Silly man, do you think a love like this
Will ever come your way?
Do you believe that what you're doing
Is reason to make her stay?
You can't love that way;
A heart that special you don't dare to play.
Look at that face and know
That you treasure the time in her place.
Be all that she needs;
Be the end of that chase.
The end of the look;
The final chapter of her look for love.
Put her in the comfort of hugs
And affectionate kisses.
Give the feeling that, now,
There's absolutely nothing missing.

Do You Know Me

Allow me to reintroduce myself.

My name's Pop J to the PB.

I've been associated with crotch wetness in ladies panties.

They can't stand me, so they just lay their asses down.

Spead wide open in preparation for a cookie pound.

The way we gets down, our conversations during penetration

Consist of the Ooowww Ahhh sound.

I'm looking to hit as I open the spit on her pithers mound.

Sooo fat so brown, no choice but to feel I'm winning,

Hearing that clapping sound.

I'm The Captain

I plays pitty pat

With her kitty cat.

The way I pounds her pussy,

She knows exactly where the dog's at.

I climbs her fuckin' back;

That's where I find the best fuckin's at.

I guess I'm a back climber.

The way I be knockin' down walls,

Maybe, I'm a vagina designer

Or a miner the way I be diggin' her well.

Such attention to detail when it comes to the tail;

Or maybe, I'm a sailor the way I makes the man in da boat set sail.

She Made Me Change

Oh, how I miss her.

I can't dismiss the thought of just kissing her.

Wherever she's at, I wish I were.

Oh, I wish I was in the middle of her hugs;

In the midst of her love.

To me, she's all of the above on a whole other level

But maintains that balance.

A lady 24/7 it comes as no challenge.

For her, I've made changes;

Being King to her Queen does have its advantages.

I've got but one life to live,

And it's most valuable moments

I've chosen to make hers to give.

My Beautiful World

I paint pictures through words,

And God has blessed me with an unlimited supply of paint,

A brush that never dries,

And the world as a canvas.

Acknowledgements

First off, I have to thank God, for without him there is no me.

I would like to thank my mother, Jessie Brinkley. She raised myself and my sister by herself on the salary of a city job, and we never wanted for anything.

I'd also like to thank my Grandfather, Vernon Bobby Dasher, may he rest in peace. He instilled in me, along with my mother, that you had to work for what you wanted, and that you shouldn't be afraid to get your hands dirty.

My grandmother, Betty Dasher the back bone of the family, instilled the love of Christ in me. When I didn't want to go to church, she made me go, anyway, and now as a man, I am so thankful to her for that. My faith and belief in the Almighty has helped me through some trying times, so thank you, Nanny.

I'd also like to thank the mother of my child, Sherilyn. She saw greatness in me when I didn't see it in myself. She is raising our daughter in the south, and has molded her into a beautiful young lady. Thank you for your love and support.

My baby girl, I thank you for giving Daddy much more reason to be better. All that I do is for you. I love you with my whole being.

To the rest of my family, friends, and my sister, Amber, it's too many to name, individually. I love you and thank you for all the love and support.

My Gem Drop family, this is proof that we can do big things! Thank you for your support.

Datrooth, my partner, thanks for believing.

Tina Wright, without you none of this was possible. You saw potential in me when others just spoke of it. You helped to bring it out. Thank you from the bottom of my heart.

Last but certainly not least, Kiah; when at my lowest, you stood by me and inspired to me in so many ways. Your work ethic is amazing, and this would not be possible without you, for when I was coming up blank, without you even knowing, you have written a lot of these love lines. God placed you in my life for many reasons, and this is one of them, without question. I love you.

I also would like to acknowledge my beautiful niece, Jessica.

Who and what I am is because of all those mentioned and some who were not, but just because your name wasn't mentioned does not diminish from the fact that I love you. Thank You All!!!!!

James Brinkley is Brooklyn born and bred and remains a Brooklyn resident with ties to Douglasville Georgia. Humble as they come, as a writer, he continues to grow and searches his soul for that which he writes. Love Lines comes to his heart mainly from being raised by a single mom who told him that, as a man, he should appreciate and cherish the love of a good woman. This book is an expression of love to the women out there who don't believe a man is capable of speaking his feelings.

A man committed and dedicated to family life, James is father to one daughter and has one sibling, a sister. He is the son of a single mom who worked hard to provide the best that life had to offer to him and his sister. With cousins in abundance, there was never an absence of fun growing up in the projects of Brooklyn. Wanting to provide a better life for his daughter, James moved to Douglasville Ga. While in Georgia, he married a long time girlfriend and mother of his daughter and started a new life as a family with her and her son and daughter from previous relationships. Since then, they decided to part ways, but to this day remain good friends.

Love Lines is for the love of the ladies. He intends to prove that the good man is not just someone who is a product of imagination but someone who is real. Words mean little if the actions don't coincide with them. In no way does he claim to be the perfect man but shows that he still has growing to do for self and for the love of that special lady.

www.ingramcontent.com/pod-product-compliance
Lightning Source LLC
Chambersburg PA
CBHW070114070426
42448CB00039B/2764